MULTIPLE MINI INTERVIEW
FOR MEDICAL SCHOOL

Multiple Mini Interview for Medical School: The Essentials

Jordan Westley

Copyright © 2020 by Jordan Westley

All rights reserved.

No part of this book may be reproduced in any form or by any electronic or mechanical means including information storage and retrieval systems, without permission in writing from the author. The only exception is by a reviewer, who may quote short excerpts in a review.

Printed in United States of America

TABLE OF CONTENTS

TABLE OF FIGURES v
1. INTRODUCTION 2
2. MMI BACKGROUND 10
   Why is the traditional panel-style interview being replaced with the MMI? 10
   What is the MMI (Multiple Mini Interview)? 11
3. What to expect in an MMI? 14
   What are the MMI questions like? 18
   Interview Experience 20
4. Marking Scheme 26
   About the interviewers 32
   Prompting Questions 32
   Useful training exercise 33
5. Nuances in MMI Between Schools 34
   University of Alberta and the University of Calgary 35
   University of British Columbia 36
6. APPROACH TO ANSWERING MMI QUESTIONS 38
   What to do in the two minutes before answering the question? 39
   Posture and Body Position in the MMI Room 40
   Tips that'll be useful during the MMI 42
7. Types of MMI Questions 44
   Ethical-scenario based questions 45
   Society or current events questions 50
   Spontaneous – creative questions 51
   Getting to know you personally questions 54

Do you know the school questions 54
Delivery of the questions 55
    Direct Question 55
    Interactive Chatting Questions 55
    Interrogator and evaluator in the same room 56
    Role Playing Questions 57
Summary of Types of Questions 60

8.   PREPARATION PRIOR TO INTERVIEW 62
Three months before the interview 62
Mock MMI Practice 63
    Mock MMI Simulation Conditions 63
Training and Preparation at Home 64
    Videotape Interview Practice 64
    Posture 65
    Breathing 66
    Exercise 67
Two weeks before the interview 68

9.   Special Section for Applicants Flying Out of Town to Prepare Prior to the Interview 70
Preparation weeks before the interview 70
Preparation the day before the Interview 71
    Getting to know the city of the medical school 71
    Dinner 72
    Sleep 73
Preparations for the day of the interview 73
    Breakfast 73
    Importance of water and health snacks 74

    After the interview 74

    A checklist of things to pack when traveling to an interview 74

10.   Preparation the day before the interview 76

11.   What to wear for the multiple mini interview? 78

12.   The day of the interview 80

13.   After the interview 82

14.   CONCLUSION 84

FULL LENGTH MMI PRACTICE EXAM 86

Comments for MMI Questions 122

Interviewer Scoring Sheets 128

NOTES 132

iii

TABLE OF FIGURES

Figure 1 Diagram of MMI name tag.. 14
Figure 2 Layout of multiple mini interview 15
Figure 3 Typical MMI testing facility 16
Figure 4 Typical multiple mini interview room 17
Figure 5 Layout of MMI Room... 23
Figure 6 Example of an MMI Marking Scheme.. 26
Figure 7 Example of the evaluation sheet used by the interviewer 28

1. INTRODUCTION

I'll strive the get across the essence or the most important aspects of the MMI as simple as possible. The MMI can be made to be too complicated and stressful. Especially in high stress environments, it is most important to keep things simple to minimize the chances of error. If you keep to the basics, you will do surprisingly well. I think the biggest thing is the stress of the situation decreases the performance for too many applicants. The other thing is people often over think or complicate the process. I will explain the big picture, important parts and structure to keep in mind. Then explain the details throughout the rest of the book. The most important things to keep in mind is to understand the big picture. According to Pareto's principle, 90% of the results is due to only 10% of the work. The hard part is knowing the 10% you should be focusing your efforts. Often, we figure out the 10% after a lot trial and error and wish we had known it from the beginning. It is this experience and insight gained through time, trial and reflection that is valuable and when distilled into the essence results in expertise that appears facile and with ease. I hope to make the future applicant's life easier by imparting experience and insight gained through trial and error so you don't have to figure things out and have a smoother path in the future.

The questions they can create for the MMI is unlimited, but they are really testing your ability to formulate a sensible response and to filter out applicants with red flags. Most people will formulate an acceptable answer and honestly most people sound very similar to the interviewer. So, most people will score in the middle. There are a few people who score exceptionally well and a few people who score exceptionally low or state questionable things that may be unethical. If you score within the middle, your chances of getting in are already quite high. So, putting everything into perspective, you shouldn't be too stressed about interview. Understandably, there will be stress on the day due to having to go through the process. That is why it is important to be prepared and practiced through this book.

There are questions that will ask you for an opinion, stance, or debate an issue that is current based on medical issues, non-medical issues or current events. The key to these types of questions is to articulate the issue and define any terms if necessary. Then explain the pros and cons of each situation or issue. Then conclude with a summary of the pros and cons and any limitations in reaching a definitive conclusion. Articulate the factors you would need to consider in order to help you decide on which position is better. Usually, the topics are too complex to definitively stand on a side and have many factors to consider. And you truly don't have enough information to have a strong stance. But it is important that you understand the issue and factors to consider in order to reach a conclusion. Often, it depends on certain circumstances and individual considerations and the answer depends on the individual and circumstances at the time. The important point of the question is that the answer is logical and considers all the important factors. By using this approach, the response will sound sensible, intelligent, organized, and comprehensive. Having an approach in mind will keep you calm by knowing regardless of the question, you know how to deal with it. By practicing the questions, your mind will get used to the format and approach. Even when presented with a topic that you're not entirely knowledgeable about, you can admit your limitations and discuss the factors that come to mind and possible sources of information you can use to search for the information you need. You will still do reasonably well on the question even when you don't know the topic well. The few people that do exceptionally well will be more knowledgeable about the topic than most and use the approach we discussed. But that is not necessary to perform well enough on the interviews to be admitted. Different people will be more knowledgeable or prepared for different questions or topics and it is rare for a person to be exceptionally knowledgeable on all the topics in the entire interview. It levels the playing field for the applicants by having a wide variety of different questions and topics. While you're preparing for the interview by practicing the approach, it is helpful to concurrently read about current events, basic medical ethics, and understand the Royal College of Physicians and Surgeons CanMEDS Framework. There will also be questions that are on topics or fictional scenarios that you can't really prepare by background reading and will rely on the approach we talked about.

The reading of current events does not need to be extensive but to serve the purpose of in case they raise an issue that is related to current events, it helps to be at least aware of the issues. They may not have a question about current events, so you do not need to put a lot of effort in this regard.

You only need a basic understanding of medical ethics. Being ethical in the response is primary. It helps to be more articulate if you've done some reading about it by using a few of the terms and topics in answering the question. "Doing Right" by Philip C. Hébert is a book that can be read to give a strong foundation. In case you don't have time to read the book, I'll summarize a few key points. The core of medical ethics is based on four principles which Doing Right goes in detail to explain each principle. Ideally, for a medical practice to be considered "ethical", it must respect all four of these principles: autonomy, beneficence, non-maleficence, and justice. Autonomy is respecting the patient's right to make decisions regarding their body and health. The decision-making process must be free of coercion or coaxing. In order for a patient to make a fully informed decision, she/he must understand all risks and benefits of the procedure and the likelihood of success. Beneficence is doing good for the patient. Non-maleficence is not harming the patient. Justice is equitable use of societal resources and not wasting societal resources. All ethical issues can be assessed using this framework, so it is a useful framework to use when dealing with ethical questions. Examples of applying the framework to various medical ethical issues are discussed in detail with the Doing Right book.

Physicians are evaluated on seven roles under a structure called CanMEDS developed by the Royal College of Physicians and Surgeons. Some questions may target one or more of these roles with opportunities to bring examples from your own life that support these roles or scenarios that you could answer that focus on these roles. So, it is helpful to be aware of the CanMEDS roles by reading about the CanMEDS roles on the Royal College of Physicians and Surgeons website (http://www.royalcollege.ca/rcsite/canmeds/canmeds-framework-e). You can prepare by thinking of examples with personal stories/events in your life that exemplifies each of the CanMEDS roles so you can provide an example in case there is a question about it. At the very least, awareness of CanMEDS will let you identify the question as targeting one of these roles and cues you into what they want or are asking. I'll explain CanMEDS briefly so at least you have an idea if you don't have time to review the website. The CanMEDS roles includes:

Medical Expert (the integrating role)

Communicator

Collaborator

Leader

Health Advocate

Scholar

Professional

The roles have overlap with the central role being the medical expert. The medical expert is the main purpose of medical school which is to develop the knowledge and experience in practicing medicine. The interview question may be a medical topic but will not expect you to have medical expertise because they know that you are applying to get into medical school to learn the medical knowledge and it is unfair to assume medical knowledge prior to admission.

Communicator is communicating to patients, other physicians, and allied health care professionals. Communication is a relatively easy role to test in interviews because it doesn't necessarily require medical knowledge. They can ask for examples of communication such as an example when you had to deal with conflict and how you managed it.

Collaborator is collaborating or working with other people usually as part of the healthcare team including nurses, allied healthcare professionals, physicians, and patient. But also, can include collaborating with other stakeholders in public health policy at different levels of government. This can be tested in an interview by asking the applicant about their experience with working in a team.

Leader is when physicians engage with others to contribute to a vision of a high-quality health care system and take responsibility for the delivery of excellent patient care through their activities as clinicians, administrators, scholars, or teachers. Being a leader doesn't mean they are always right, dominating, in control, or at the head of the team. Sometimes, being a leader means they need to take a smaller role for the greater good of the team. Being a leader also means knowing one's limitations and getting other people to help. They may ask a question related to leadership and you can support it with an example in your life in which you were involved in a leadership role or witnessing someone else demonstrating a good example of leadership that you learned from them.

Health advocate is when physicians contribute their expertise and influence as they work with communities or patient populations to improve health. They work with those they serve to determine and understand needs, speak on behalf of others when required, and support the mobilization of resources to effect change. Being a health advocate can take on different levels ranging from an individual personal level, to a team level, to a governmental level. It can be as simple as speaking on behalf of the patient to other specialists or health care professionals. It can also be thinking of the issues from the patient's perspective and helping to resolve them before issues arise, such as deliberately arranging for bubble packed medications to help with keeping multiple medications sorted. It can also be about requesting for public health policy changes at the governmental level that will help issues faced by patients.

Scholar is when physicians demonstrate a lifelong commitment to excellence in practice through continuous learning and by teaching others, evaluating evidence, and contributing to scholarship. Basically, it is about research, teaching and education. This is where research experience prior to medical school can play a role if there is an opportunity to talk about your research experience. Understanding evidence-based medicine as a concept can be helpful for other types of interview questions. The key point about understanding evidence-based medicine as a concept is knowing that it is practicing Medicine using the best available evidence based on medical research. It involves medical research that is assessed based on the strength of the evidence and applied to the patient's condition. An example question could be asking about alternative medicine such as herbal medicine and its role with traditional Western Medicine. Using the evidence-based medicine concept and scholar role, a response could include evaluating alternative medicine under the same criteria of research through clinical trials as in Western medicine. Incorporate alternative medicine as the evidence from research support it. Allow use of alternative medicine if there is no harm to the patient. Recommend alternative medicine as supported by evidence-based medicine.

Professional is when physicians are committed to the health and well-being of individual patients and society through ethical practice, high personal standards of behavior, accountability to the profession and society, physician-led regulation, and maintenance of personal health. The professional role is where questions of ethics can appear. A current issue about professionalism is acting professional in real life and on social media along with the difficulty of separating your professional life from your personal life on social media. Inappropriate behavior and lack of professionalism on social media have been problematic for people's professional life even though it was done during their personal life.

We have talked about the key concepts to keep in mind when preparing for the multiple mini interview. Review this section to consolidate the information as you read through the rest of the book, as you practice your interviews, and get closer to the interview.

2. MMI BACKGROUND

Why is the traditional panel-style interview being replaced with the MMI?

The traditional panel-style interview has no evidence that it will predict the success of candidates upon completion of medical school. Studies started from McMaster University have provided evidence that the multiple mini interviews are better than the traditional panel-style interview in predicting the success of selected candidates for medical school. The MMI has numerous strengths which led to several of the Canada's medical schools to adopt it as a tool for selecting students. The MMI allows multiple samples of insight into a candidate's abilities and the MMI dilutes the effect of chance and examiner bias. The MMI can be standardized by having MMI stations structured so that all candidates respond to the same questions and interviewers receive background information a priori. There is virtually an infinite selection of questions that can be created giving MMI exam developers the ability to create MMI stations that can be designed with a great deal of flexibility to select students with the personal attributes desired by the medical school. Candidates can feel confident they will be given a chance to recover from a disastrous station by moving to a new, independent reviewer. Scientific studies have assessed the effectiveness of the MMI and the MMI has been found to better predict pre-clerkship OSCE performance than assessment of non- academic traits by autobiographical submissions, the standard panel interview, or simulated tutorial. In short, the MMI is a work in progress but has already been shown to be valid, reliable, and fairer in comparison to the traditional interview. The basic concept is to provide a standardized interview format regarding the questions asked and method of evaluation.

What is the MMI (Multiple Mini Interview)?

The MMI is an innovation in medical school interviews that is drastically different from the traditional interview. The MMI was developed in 2003 at McMaster University and used to select students in 2004. The Northern Ontario Medical School following in 2005 and in 2008 all five Western Canadian medical schools and five Eastern Canadian medical schools used the MMI.

Most Canadian schools now use MMI. The University of British Columbia, University of Alberta, University of Calgary, University of Saskatchewan, University of Manitoba, Northern Ontario Medical School, Dalhousie University, Memorial University, McGill University, and McMaster Medical School all use the MMI. Previously, the opposite was true, only McMaster and the University of Calgary used the MMI and the rest of the Canadian medical schools continued to use the traditional interview. Australian medical schools are now also using the MMI.

The multiple mini interview (MMI) is a series of short, structured interviews used to assess personal traits/qualities. Each mini interview provides a candidate with two minutes to read a question/scenario and mentally prepare before entering the interview room. Upon entering, the candidate has eight minutes of dialogue with one interviewer/assessor (or, in some cases, a third party as the interviewer/assessor observes). At the conclusion of the interview, the interviewer/assessor uses the next two-minute period to complete the evaluation form while the candidate moves to the next scenario. This pattern is repeated through a circuit of 10 stations, taking 100 – 120 minutes (depending on number of rest stations built in). The MMI was derived from the well- known OSCE (objective structured clinical examination) used by most undergraduate medical programs to assess a student's application of clinical skills and knowledge. Note: The MMI differs from the OSCE in that the MMI is neither clinical nor objective.

3. What to expect in an MMI?

The candidates arrive in a room (collecting room) where they will receive a name tag and will be explained the process of the MMI. The name tag will have a number that will indicate the order or room in which you begin answering the MMI questions. On the name tag, the MMI group that you belong will also be written and the group is usually labeled by a color. Also, on the name tag is your name and photograph of you.

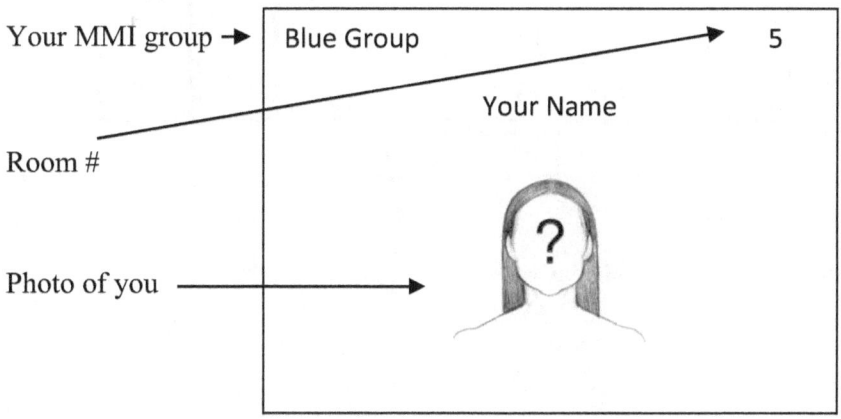

Figure 1 Diagram of MMI name tag

The applicants will line up according to the number assigned and written on the name tag. There will be about 8 to 10 questions so there will be about 8 to 10 applicants per group. The number of questions varies between the schools, but most have 8 questions and some have 2 rest stations in addition to the questions where the applicant can rest.

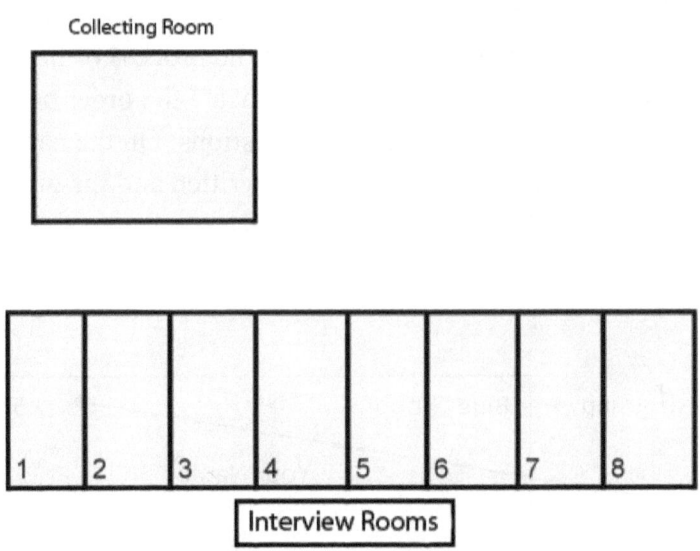

Figure 2 Layout of multiple mini interview

The applicants will be taken from the collecting room to a long hallway with many rooms that are numbered.

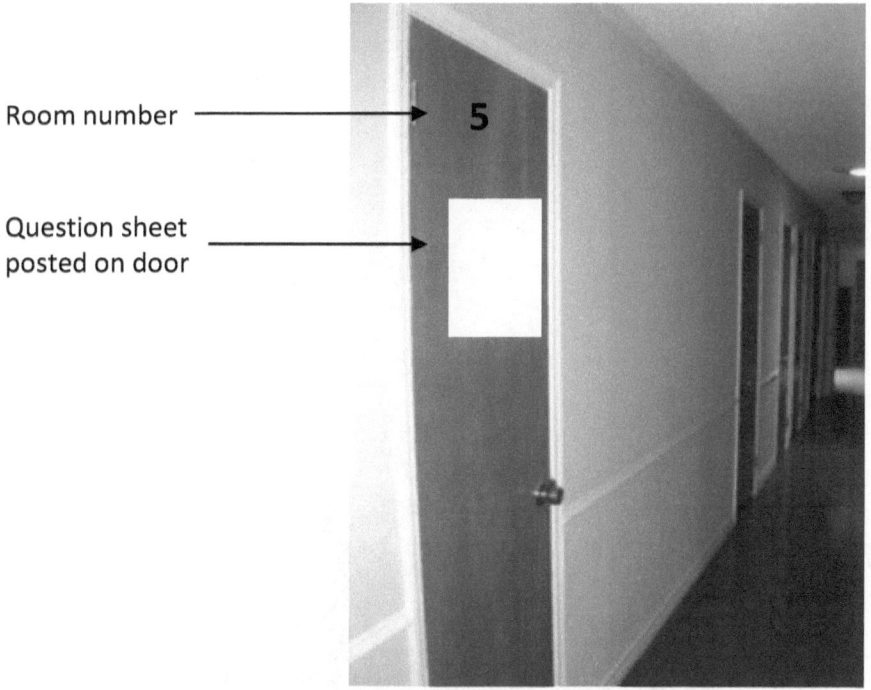

Figure 3 Typical MMI testing facility

Each room will have one interview question. The applicants stand in front of the room labeled with the same number that was assigned to them. A bell will ring, and the applicant can read the question posted on the door of the room. The applicant will have two minutes to read and think about the question. A bell will ring at the end of the two minutes to signal the applicants to stop reading the question and to enter the room to answer the question.

Figure 4 Typical multiple mini interview room

An interviewer will be inside the room. The applicant will have 8 to 10 minutes to answer the question depending on the medical school. A bell will ring to signal the time limit to answer the question and the applicant will leave the room. The interviewer will fill out the evaluation form for the applicant when the applicant leaves the room. The applicant moves to the next door and begins reading the question for two minutes and the cycle is repeated until the applicant answers all the questions. As you progress through the questions, there may be one or more rest stations in which you can sit and rest for the time allotted for one interview question.

What are the MMI questions like?
MMI questions are usually a scenario that you can easily relate to and culminates with a specific question for you to answer. The scenarios are clearly written and unambiguous. The preamble is less 100 words. There are no correct answers and there will be enough material for you to talk for eight minutes.

There will be prompting questions, and these are a series of questions, usually three to five questions, designed to help you if you require it. The prompting questions are not provided to you but are given as a list to the interviewer. You can ask the interviewer for the prompting questions or the interviewer can offer them to you if they feel it would help you. Usually the interviewer will ask you the prompting questions after you finish your initial response. The prompting questions are provided one at a time and the interviewer is not allowed to deviate from the list of questions and so some of the questions may ask for things you have already mentioned in your initial answer.

An example of an MMI question used at the MMI for McMaster's medical school is shown below.

> Dr Cheung recommends homeopathic medicines to his patients. There is no scientific evidence or widely accepted theory to suggest that homeopathic medicines work, and Dr Cheung

doesn't believe them to. He recommends homeopathic medicine to people with mild and non-specific symptoms such as fatigue, headaches and muscle aches, because he believes that it will do no harm, but will give them reassurance.

Consider the ethical problems that Dr Cheung's behaviour might pose. Discuss these issues with the interviewer.

The interviewer will be holding a sheet of prompting questions that he or she may ask at the end of your response. An example of prompting questions for the above questions is:

- What's wrong with the way Dr. Cheung treats his patients? Why is that wrong?
- Why do you think Dr. Cheung does it?
- Can you see any circumstances under which recommending a placebo might be the appropriate action?
- What is the difference between the applicant's previous response and Dr. Cheung's practice?
- What action would you take regarding Dr. Cheung?

Interview Experience

Narrative of a typical MMI experience from the applicant's perspective

The feeling while you wait for the bell to begin in the MMI

You will arrive at the medical school and walk along the entrance hallway following the signs to the registration booth. At the registration booth you provide the documents the school has sent and had requested you to complete to be submitted at the day of the interview. In exchange for the documents you will receive a name tag to hang around your neck and it might even have a photo of you that you submitted earlier by e-mail and a page full of small stickers that have your name and a number printed on each sticker. You are told to sit in a common area full of seats and other applicants dressed in dark suits also wearing name tags and holding stickers and waiting. There is a table full of water bottles that you can take before finding a seat. If you're lucky, there will be some current medical students available to chat with you to reassure you to not be nervous and to answer any questions you might have about the medical school and program. The medical student disclaims that nothing you discuss with him or her will affect your admission. You will probably chat with a few fellow applicants and medical students. You have about ten or twenty minutes before the MMI orientation begins and you're allowed to use the washroom to freshen up and relieve any nervous energy. Most people go to the washroom, so they won't need to during the interview. You look at your sheet of stickers and wonder what it is used for. The time for the interview orientation approaches and you are split into a group of about ten people, given a number and color that you realize is printed on your stickers and name tag and line up in a predetermined number sequence. The orientation leader explains the instructions of the MMI and the purpose of the stickers.

Instructions for the MMI:

The interview orientation leader will verbally describe the instructions and may have a PowerPoint presentation as part of the explanation.

There will be eight applicants and a leader who will meet in the collecting room where you wait and receive instructions. Then you will be taken to the interview rooms and you stand in front of the door that you have been assigned. A bell will ring and you will have 2 minutes to read the question at which time another bell will ring to signal the end of the 2 minutes. Then you can enter the room and begin your interview with the interviewer. You will have 8 minutes in the interview room with interviewer when another bell will ring to signal the end of the station. Then you will proceed to the next room and have another 2 minutes to read the question. This will continue until all the stations are complete. Then you will return to the room in which we had the orientation for a short debriefing.

The stickers are to be given to the interviewer at each station. The interviewer will place the sticker on your evaluation sheet. It is important that you remember to give the sticker to each interviewer, the orientation leader reminds everyone. The orientation leader suggests that everyone pre-lift the corner of each sticker to make it easier for you to remove the sticker for the interviewer as every candidate will invariably be nervous and fumbles with the sticker as he or she tries to give the sticker to the interviewer. After the explanation of the MMI procedure, all the applicants wait in the lineup for the group leaders to bring the applicants to the interview rooms. The applicants are taken to a narrow hallway full of doors with paper taped on the door and seats in front of each door. The applicants are led down the hallway of doors and stand in front of the door with the number that corresponds with the number on their name tag. The applicants are told to stand with their backs to the door and not to read the sheet of paper taped on the door. The applicants stare across the hallway and at other applicants who are staring back and waiting. This is the nervous and awkward part of the interview when you may notice nervous applicants taking deep breaths and crossing their hearts. You wait for the bell to ring to start the first question of the series of multiple mini interviews. The bell finally rings, and you turn around to read the question. You read the question and ponder about the question and think about what to say to the interviewer. You look around and all the applicants are staring intently at the door and reading the question. Some applicants are dancing around while they're thinking and oblivious to everyone and everything else while others are frantically writing notes. You finished reading the question with plenty of time to spare and have thought of almost everything you could think of and the bell rings. You open the door to enter a small room with white walls, no windows, and a small table in the middle and a chair on either side.

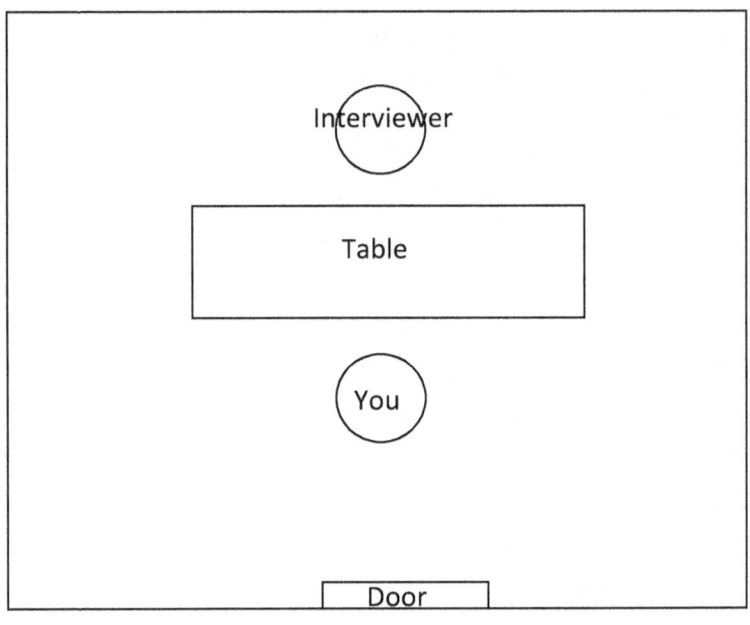

Figure 5 Layout of MMI Room

The interviewer is sitting in the far chair behind the table and gets up as you say hello and you walk towards her to shake her hand. She invites you to sit down and asks for your sticker. You fumble to find the sticker and peel just one sticker to the interviewer who takes the sticker and places it on a blank evaluation sheet. You wait for the interviewer to start the interview and she smiles and looks back and asks if you had a chance to read the question. The interviewer points to a sheet of paper on the desk that is a photocopy of the question sheet that was on the door. You reply that you have had a chance to look at the question and she invites you to start whenever you're ready. You talk about everything you thought of outside of the room and you managed to fill a few minutes. But there are several more minutes left, and the interviewer asks a question and you are inspired to talk some more until you have finished expressing your thoughts. The interviewer again asks another question and you talk again. Now that you're done talking the interviewer asks if you have anything else you would like to add and invites you to look at the question sheet again if you want. You look at the question sheet again but can't think of anything else to add. She tells you that's okay and that we'll just wait for the bell to signal the end of the station. You remember you were told in the interview orientation that you're not allowed to talk to the interviewer about anything other than the question and that the interviewer will not respond to any attempts at conversation even if there is an awkward silence. The interviewer smiles at you as you stare back at her while you wait for the station to end. There is a pitcher of ice water and a stack of plastic cups. You pour yourself a cup of water and didn't realize how thirsty you really felt until the soothing cold water coats your tongue. You look around the room as a distraction to the awkward silence. Suddenly the buzzer rings to signal the end of the station and you feel a sense of relief and pop out of the chair, shake the interviewer's hand and thank the interviewer while you rush out of the room. You close the door and see the applicant in the next door come out and rush to the next room. You rush to the next room to maximize the time to read and think about the next question because you know the buzzer that signaled the end of the question also signaled the beginning of the two minutes to read the next question. You continue this sequence again for another three stations and you begin to feel tired but the nervous and anxious energy begins to subside as you get into the swing of things and feel like you know how things work. If you're lucky, the university has a rest station at about the half way point. At the rest station you get to sit and relax for eight minutes, use the washroom and maybe chat with a medical student. Then you continue again through another four stations. As you near the end of the stations you begin to count and look forward to the last station. You feel tired and want to get the stations done as you near the second to last station. When you finish all the stations you feel a sense of relief. You feel surprised that it is all over and it wasn't as bad or long as you thought. As you move out to the resting area you start to feel tired mentally and physically. The adrenaline begins to wear off and you start to think that the MMI lasted for a long time. But you do the math and it was only for an hour and a half. You overhear some other applicants talking out loud about feeling tired from the interview and feel a sense of relief. You realize that you weren't the only person who felt this way. As you enter the rest area to fill out evaluation forms, a lady walks around with a plate of cookies and you gladly take a cookie to fuel yourself with sugar and a treat for finishing the multiple mini interviews. The interviews are done, and you are free to go home or to continue to attend the activities and tours planned by the school.

4. Marking Scheme

The MMI's are marked on a scale, usually 1 to 5, sometimes 1 to 10, 1 to 4, or 1 to 3 depending on the school. The interviewers are encouraged to use as much of the scale as possible to create clear distinctions between applicants. In general, the interviewers are considering the strength of the arguments and answer; ability to communicate clearly, concisely, and in an organized manner; the applicant's suitability as a physician; and the overall impression of the applicant and response. An example of an MMI marking scheme is shown below and is used by the University of Alberta.

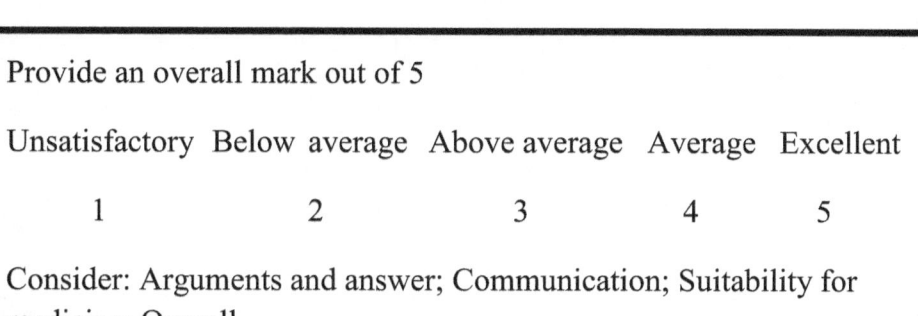

Figure 6 Example of an MMI Marking Scheme

Another example of an MMI evaluation sheet used by the interviewers is shown below. This evaluation sheet is from McMaster's medical school. The important thing to note is that the evaluation sheet is still looking at a few broad categories and the applicants are ranked on a scale of relative performance. The sample evaluation sheet below has more basic information shown on the sheet including the name of applicant and interviewer, interview question, and potential conflict of interest.

STATION 1

SCORE SHEET

Applicant's Name: _____   Potential Conflict of Interest?: Y N

Interviewer's Name: _____   If "Yes," Why? _____

> Dr. Blair recommends homeopathic medicines to his patients. There is no scientific evidence or widely accepted theory to suggest that homeopathic medicines work, and Dr. Blair doesn't believe them to. He recommends homeopathic medicine to people with mild and non-specific symptoms such as fatigue, headaches, and muscle aches, because he believes that it will do no harm, but will give them reassurance.
>
> Consider the ethical problems that Dr. Blair's behaviour might pose. Discuss these issues with the interviewer.

Please rate the following aspects of this applicant's performance <u>on this station relative to the pool of all applicants you are rating</u>. You may adjust your scores as necessary before turning them in.

1. Please score the communication skills the applicant displayed during this station

Bottom 25%	Top 75%	Top 50%	Top 35%	Top 25%	Top 15%	Top 10%	Top 5%	Top 3%	Top 1%	NA
Worst Applicant									Best Applicant	

2. Please score the strength of the applicant's arguments presented during this station

Bottom 25%	Top 75%	Top 50%	Top 35%	Top 25%	Top 15%	Top 10%	Top 5%	Top 3%	Top 1%	NA

3. Based on this brief encounter, please rate the **applicant's suitability for a career in medicine**

Bottom 25%	Top 75%	Top 50%	Top 35%	Top 25%	Top 15%	Top 10%	Top 5%	Top 3%	Top 1%	NA

<u>Please score the applicant's overall performance on this station</u>

Bottom 25%	Top 75%	Top 50%	Top 35%	Top 25%	Top 15%	Top 10%	Top 5%	Top 3%	Top 1%	NA

Comments:

Figure 7 Example of the evaluation sheet used by the interviewer

Please note that an applicant scoring unsatisfactory in one checklist item does not mean the applicant has failed. An applicant doing poorly in one section can be compensated for by doing well in other sections.

The table below provides a guideline for assessors in assigning grades in the MMI.

Table 1 Guidelines for assigning grades in the MMI

Excellent	As for the criteria for 'Good' however the applicant shows a degree of originality and creativity in the applicant's answer. There is evidence of the ability to generalize the subject content to areas not covered in the formal scenario. There is strong evidence of critical reflection on professionalism of both themselves and that of others. There is identification of strategies for how they themselves and others might behave in the given circumstances. The answers appear authentic.
Average	The work shows a good appreciation of the general issues in the context of professionalism. There is good coverage of the topic with relevant and reasoned argument. The answers demonstrate a clear view of how the various aspects of the topic relate to one another. There is reasonable evidence of critical reflection on professionalism of both themselves and that of others. The answers appear authentic.
Below Average	The answers are relevant, but do not address all aspects of the topic. There is demonstration of understanding of the issue being considered and just enough evidence that a reasonable argument has been advanced. There is evidence of critical reflection on professionalism of both themselves and that of others but the answers are more descriptive, than analytical. The answers indicate a modest understanding of the topic but appear authentic.
Unsatisfactory	The discussion of the issue is not always relevant and accurate and key points may have been omitted. There is doubtful evidence of any clear strategies to guide how they should behave or others should. There is an attempt at reasoned argument, but of doubtful quality. There is insufficient reflection on the behaviours of themselves or others. Sometimes the answers appears contrived.

Some of the attributes that may be considered during the evaluation center around qualities desired in a health care professional. Some of the attributes are outlined and described below.

Integrity
Being of good character requires a person to have moral courage and demonstrate traits of honesty and virtue. Honesty or truth telling is an important moral value that in health care refers to the duty of a health professional to tell the truth and an unwillingness to tell lies.

Respect for Diversity
The concept of diversity encompasses acceptance and mutual respect for qualities and experiences that are different from one's own. These can be along the dimensions of race, ethnicity, gender, sexual orientation, socio-economic status, age, physical abilities, religious beliefs, political beliefs.

Sensitive to the Needs of others and establish rapport
Aware of and responsive to the feelings of others. Virtues of kindness, empathy and benevolence. Recognize the emotional and physical vulnerability of the human condition. Understanding these difficulties and being able to respond sensitively and appropriately are essential qualities in health practitioners.

Self-Control
Control or restraint of oneself or one's actions, feelings, etc.

Tact and Diplomacy
Tact: A keen sense of what to say or do to avoid giving offence; skill in dealing with difficult or delicate situations. Diplomacy: Skill in managing negotiations, handling people, etc., so that there is little or no ill will.

Conscientiousness
Characterized by showing care, attention, and effort

Effective communicator
The ability to convey information and ideas clearly is a central facet of safe and effective health care. Listening and verbal skills are essential components of effective communication.

Demonstrates insight

The appreciation of the role of one's values and attitudes and the capacity to recognize and change behaviors that impede personal and professional growth and development

Effective decision maker
The capacity to make a decision based on the available information, know how to tackle a problem, and how to identify the steps in problem solving

Information manager
Knowing how to record and recall information. The ability to sift information and summarize the most important issues is central to being an effective practitioner.

Ability to make a shared plan
Health care services are best delivered by teams of people working collaboratively. The ability to share information, make shared decisions with patients and other members of the health care team is key to optimizing health outcomes.

Self-directed learner
The capacity to impose self-discipline and an inquiring mind to further knowledge and skills

Understands the role of health professionals in society
The success of twenty-first century medicine largely corresponds with scientific research and discoveries. Understanding the benefits of science as well as the pressures to clinical practice are important for understanding the role of medicine in society.

About the interviewers

The interviewers have been trained by the medical school about a week prior to the interview. In general, the training provides background and evaluation information on the medical school, admission and interview and includes a brief overview of the current curricula, overview of the admission procedures to the medical school program, practical aspects of being an interviewer in the MMI, and applying the scoring system. Each interviewer will only evaluate one question and will repeatedly evaluate many applicants and their responses to the single question they were assigned. The initial few applicants of the interview period will set the expectation for the interviewers. The interviewers are generally medical students, faculty, and community members and you will not know the background of the interviewers. The interviews will introduce themselves by their name, so for example, John Smith instead of Dr. Smith or Professor Smith.

Prompting Questions

The use of the prompting question may affect your evaluation. Prompting questions help the applicant to cover the different points of the question and allow the applicant a fair opportunity to show the applicant's thinking. If the applicant does not use the prompting questions as a crutch to get them to answer the question, then the applicant should not be penalized. In general, the applicant should try their best to answer the question and use the prompting questions when necessary.

Useful training exercise

It is a useful exercise to ask a few friends or family to practice answering MMI questions and for you to evaluate them. There is insight that can be gained by you being the evaluator of someone else. You should video record the interview, preferable at an angle to view both the interviewer and the responder. By going through the evaluation on someone else, you will gain insight on the thought process of the interviewer and this will give you a better understanding of things interviewers would be evaluating. When you view the video of the interview, you will notice your own facial reactions as an interviewer in response the answers of the other person. You can gain insight on the facial expressions of yourself as an interviewer and what you thought of at the time when you listened to another person answering the question. But you may also realize that you may inadvertently reveal facial expressions of boredom from listening to someone answering the same question a few times and realize it is not directly reflective of the applicant's answer but more due to your personal boredom. You can objectively learn from the strength and weaknesses of the responder's body posture/language, delivery, and answer. Video recording yourself practicing and answering MMI questions is also a good exercise.

5. Nuances in MMI Between Schools

Although the MMI is similar in concept, the implementation varies between the schools, and there are nuances that make every MMI different between the schools. In order to give you an idea of the differences in implementation of the MMI, we will go through a couple of schools. In general, the differences are greater between schools that are further apart in the east and west direction. Schools on the west side of Canada tend to have interviewers that don't show emotions, don't respond, or won't engage in small talk during the interview. The opposite is true as you move eastward across Canada where the interviews may have similar questions, but the interviewers are more willing to show emotions, respond to the applicant's response and engage in small talk. The differences are highlighted by comparing the University of Alberta and the University of Calgary in Alberta to the University of British Columbia in British Columbia which are the two most Western Canadian provinces. Both are neighboring provinces and should have the most similarity in MMI implementation, but we will see that there are differences between them. The MMI implementation changes every year and the provided examples are used to illustrate the point. Please refer to the website for each school for the latest interview information.

University of Alberta and the University of Calgary

The interview at the University of Alberta has evolved since they first introduced the MMI. The first time they introduced the MMI, they followed the protocol of other western Canadian schools but had a couple more questions and a minute longer interview time per question than UBC. But it was still shorter than U of C. The subsequent year, U of A maintained a similar format but reacted to the feedback of the lack of personal interaction in the MMI structure and changed the MMI to include two addition pass/fail questions where a person will have a conversation to get to know you better at the beginning and end of the interview. U of A appears to enjoy creating very creative questions that require more spontaneous thinking than the other schools. U of A and U of C both allow for note taking before each question using the provided pencil and paper.

The number of questions or stations varies between the University of Calgary and the University of Alberta. In the University of Calgary, the verbal MMI consists of 9 stations. At each station, you are given 2 minutes to read the scenario, then 8 minutes with the interviewer. While in the University of Alberta there are 10 stations plus 2 additional interactive stations where an interviewer will chat with the applicant for 8 minutes.

The University of Calgary also has an additional written MMI station where you write two essays based on essay questions, statistics, articles, and pictures provided in a booklet. The essays are done on computer. The University of Calgary is the only school in Canada that has a written MMI station. A written MMI station will be held at the Library Commons in the Health Science Centre. You will be given 2 questions and have 60 minutes to complete your written answers. You will be responsible for managing your time appropriately. Please do not take food or drink into the computer area. You may want to bring ear plugs in case you have difficulty concentrating with 35 other typing applicants. Please refer to the University of Calgary website for the latest information.

University of British Columbia

The University of British Columbia has a more just business approach to the MMI. There is less of a preamble and more get in, start the interview and leave approach than U of A and U of C. Any presentations or social events for the applicants are at a separate time and venue. There are no pencils or paper allowed to write down your thoughts for each question, so all your mental preparation must be done in your head. Please refer to the University of British Columbia for the latest information.

6. APPROACH TO ANSWERING MMI QUESTIONS

Some people use pencil and paper to write down their ideas during the two minutes provided to read the question. Other people don't write down their ideas and formulate their ideas in their mind. This is a personal preference and depends on which you are most comfortable. There are advantages of not using paper and pencil because not all schools provide it. The two minutes prior to answering the question is used to read the question, calm down, and brainstorm ideas that come to mind when you read the question. Then go in with some ideas that you've thought of and let them flow forward. Using pencil and paper to jot down ideas requires time that is limited. Furthermore, some people may be restricted by the ideas written and may not flow as naturally. Without the restrictions of the paper and pen, ideas are more natural, engaging, persuasive and can change with reaction of the interviewer if they reveal anything or ask follow-up questions. These other elements are important in the MMI because they are also measuring the softer skills of communication and add to the overall impression of the candidate. Hence, it is important to be relaxed, natural and communicate persuasively, logically, and in an organized manner.

What to do in the two minutes before answering the question?

During the two minutes given to read the question, the amount of time spent reading the question will be very short. The rest of the time should be used to think and brainstorm ideas that come to mind when you read the question. While you're thinking, you should be taking deep breaths to calm yourself and keep yourself relaxed. If you have the jitters and want to move, now is the time to move around on the spot to make you feel in your zone while you're thinking. You don't need to worry about other people seeing you because everyone else will be doing their own thing and being focused on answering their own question. You might even inspire other people to relax and be themselves while their thinking about their own question.

When you're running low on ideas, it is a good idea to read the question again to see if it will inspire more ideas and to make sure that you are really answering the question that is being asked. Sometimes there are questions that are aimed to test if you read and answer the question being asked. When you've exhausted your ideas and you feel your time is running low, you should try to summarize the entire passage into one sentence as the question being asked and have that in mind when you're walk into the room and to recall that as the question and goal while you're in the room answering the question. Framing the question into one sentence focuses you when you answer the question and makes sure you won't forget the question or go off track. You are able to read the question while you're in the room, but you don't want to be wasting time or be caught off guard in that situation.

You should wear a watch when you do the interview and check periodically to make sure you have enough time or to gauge the amount of time you spent answering and preparing for questions. You should check your watch at the beginning of the two minutes, so you know how much time you have left to think and prepare for the question. The moment you are about to open the door to the room, you should have a look at your watch to get an idea of the start time and you can take a glance at your watch to see the amount of time left to answer the question. It is okay to have a minute remaining before the buzzer signals the end of the question. The minute will go by very fast and it won't seem like a long wait before the buzzer signals you to leave the room. The minute wait will be just enough time to rest after your question and to let the answer sink in for the interviewer. Check the watch to confirm that you are on track in terms of time. You don't want to end too early as you'll have a very long silence period and you will give the impression of an incomplete answer. The questions generally are designed to give you enough to talk about to fill up the allotted time. The follow up questions will generally give enough momentum to help you fill the time allotted for the question. During the silent period of waiting for the buzzer, getting a glass of water to drink is a good distraction to fill the awkward silence and it will give you a chance to calm down and to wet your tongue. Drink moderately but not too much because you won't have time to go to the washroom until you reach a break station if it is available.

Posture and Body Position in the MMI Room

While you're in the room answering questions, you should keep both feet flat on the ground and your hands neatly on your lap. Keeping your feet flat on the ground helps to maintain composure and feeling calm while being in a neutral position. Other positions such as crossing your legs will create a large physical gap between you and the interviewer which could hamper rapport and may be culturally insensitive as some cultures feel a person crossing their legs is a sign of lack of respect for the interviewer. Moreover, keeping the same body position in each interview question builds a routine, removes a factor in your thinking and ensures that you are in the correct body position each time. Placing your hands on your lap prevents your body from performing unnecessary hand gestures that may be distracting to the interviewer and detract from your message. Often the interview room is very small and excessive hand gestures may intrude on the interviewer's personal space while you think you are simply emphasizing or illustrating a point. When a very important point and natural hand gesture occurs, you can let your hands move but after you've made your point, place your hands back to your lap. This habit will filter out unnecessary hand gestures and only let the important hand gestures be expressed which will make your message much more clear and powerful.

You should have a good posture while you are sitting or standing because you will give a better impression, look and feel more confident. Good posture should be practiced at home to develop into a habit. The habit of being in a good posture allow you not be distracted by consciously reminding yourself to have proper posture and you can put all your effort into answering the MMI questions on the day of the interview. Methods to practice and improve posture at home prior to the interview are discussed in the training preparations at home section.

Eye contact with the interviewer is very important because you want to engage the interviewer. Eye contact is one of the most important factors in getting and keeping your interviewer's attention. Since you will most likely be in a small room, you don't want to stare at the interviewer or harbor hostility in your eye contact because it will be magnified in part due to the close contact and direct seating arrangement. Smiling is also very important, especially when you first enter the room and greet the interviewer. Under the stress of the environment, many people forget to smile and may even have a serious or hostile expression, which can lower the score for the applicant because the interviewer is partly looking for social skills and ability to make another person feel comfortable while communicating.

Tips that'll be useful during the MMI

Different schools have different etiquette in regard to knocking on the door before you enter the room. Some have a habit of knocking while others don't really care. The moment you enter the room, you make eye contact, greet the interviewer, give a firm handshake, remember to give the interviewer your sticker, and then sit down. Many applicants fumble when removing the stickers or forget to give the sticker to the interviewers. The interviewers often forget to remind the applicant to give them the sticker. A tip to avoid forgetting or fumbling to remove the sticker is to loosen the edges of the stickers prior to the interview when you are waiting in the waiting room. Preparing the stickers is also gives you something to do in the waiting room. You can fold the sticker sheet and place it in your pocket. Putting away the sticker sheet prevents people from playing with the sticker sheet or brewing nervousness through unnecessary nervous gestures.

When leaving the interview room, give eye contact, shake the interviewers hand, say thank you, and leave the room. You don't need to dawdle because the interviewer is expecting you leave, and you'll be wasting your time to read the next question.

Do not try to repeat or become circular when you run out of things to say as it will only make your message less clear, make you look less competent and confident, and bore and lose the attention of the interviewer. It is better to state your points and have silence while you think of your next point then to repeat your points in the hopes of finding something else to say while you search for something else to say. You can ask the interviewer for follow up questions if you are struggling to find new material to talk about.

7. Types of MMI Questions

The span of questions for the MMI can be immense and even infinite but there are always a few categories of MMI questions that students can prepare for in terms of material and framework for answering certain types of questions.

The main types of MMI questions include, ethical – scenario-based questions, society or current events questions, spontaneous – creative questions, getting to know you personally questions, and do you know the school questions. The delivery of the question can take on a few forms and include, direct question, interactive chatting, interrogator and evaluator in the same room, and role-playing questions.

Ethical-scenario based questions

Most of the ethical based questions are asked in a scenario in which you need to respond, form an opinion, or discuss and weigh both sides of the problem. It is more important to discuss the reasons, the factors involved, views of both sides and to come to the best conclusion possible. The conclusion should be based on the reasons and factors considered. The conclusion may not be perfect because they will have questions that are very contentious, controversial, and many competing factors with no easy answer. They will add competing factors to make sure that the problem is complicated enough that you won't have a simple answer. They may eventually press for a solid answer such as your decision to perform or not to perform a certain action. You may choose to withhold performing a certain action until later or more information is provided if the situation isn't urgent enough. Some examples of making a situation complicated would be a teenage girl and her dad comes to your clinic and you are the physician for the family. The father found out that the daughter was at a rave party and demands a pregnancy test for the daughter. The daughter says she only had a few drinks and is not pregnant. The daughter does not want to have a pregnancy test. The pregnancy test is invasive. Would you provide the pregnancy test? The situation is confounded by the independence of the daughter, right of the parent over the child, ability for the child to understand the procedure and consequences, invasiveness of the test, cost to society and fairness of allocation of resources. Outlining the issues is a significant aspect of answering such a question and the conflicting issues can be difficult to resolve. Nonetheless, the question asks, and the interviewer demands a decision and you will need to provide a yes or no answer in whether you will perform the test or not and the reason for the answer. There may be other considerations that have not been looked at including the opinion of the other mother, a legal consultation of the rights of the parent and the child, and facilitation of the negotiation between the father and daughter and providing time for them to resolve the issues and for the father to stabilize emotionally.

Another example of this type of question is the example MMI question used earlier to illustrate a typical MMI question. The question is shown again for your convenience.

> Dr Cheung recommends homeopathic medicines to his patients. There is no scientific evidence or widely accepted theory to suggest that homeopathic medicines work, and Dr Cheung doesn't believe them to. He recommends homeopathic medicine to people with mild and non-specific symptoms such as fatigue, headaches and muscle aches, because he believes that it will do no harm, but will give them reassurance.
>
> Consider the ethical problems that Dr Cheung's behaviour might pose. Discuss these issues with the interviewer.

Examples of prompting questions for the above questions are:
- A. What's wrong with the way Dr. Cheung treats his patients? Why is that wrong?
- B. Why do you think Dr. Cheung does it?
- C. Can you see any circumstances under which recommending a placebo might be the appropriate action?
- D. What is the difference between the applicant's previous response and Dr. Cheung's practice?
- E. What action would you take regarding Dr. Cheung?

In general, the first task in an ethical-scenario type of question is to find the issues being asked in the question and to address the issues. A good framework for ethics scenario is to consider the right of independence or autonomy of the individual, the benefit to the individual, any harm to others, and equality or fairness to society or others. A strong support for answering ethical questions is to always consult with the legal system because the law often encompasses some solution to ethical problems and a physician cannot disobey the law and work in the boundaries of the law. To better understand the ethical considerations and legal advice, there are several resources available that will analyze many common clinical ethical cases and are used by health care professionals in learning to deal with ethical problems. The first is a book written by a clinician and expert in ethics and is called "Doing Right." This book provides a framework to deal with clinical ethical problems and illustrates the analysis of these ethical problems with actual case reports. Another useful resource is a series of articles written by the Canadian Society of Physicians that discusses many common clinical ethical problems by providing a background of the problem, opinions of the issues, legal perspective of the problem and suggestions on dealing with the problem. By reading these resources you will develop a mindset in approaching ethical issues and have an idea of where the law stands on the issue. Based on the suggestions you will learn to think like a health care professional in dealing with the issues.

A discussion of the issues involved in above MMI example question was done by McMaster's medical school.

Placebos are still commonly used in research, and they have been used for centuries in clinical practice. The simple fact that Dr. Cheung uses placebos, then, is not what makes this case unpleasant. The ethical issues in this case arise because the doctor is behaving paternalistically. He is treating his patient much as a parent would treat a child, and he is deciding a course of care for the patient based on what he perceives the patient's needs to be. This entails deceiving his patients and making them do what is good for them.

Paternalism is only one model of the doctor/patient relationship. Others see the relationship as one between colleagues who share a common goal (the health of the patient), one between rational contractors (who agree on a contract leading to health), or one between a technician and a consumer of medical expertise. Each metaphor for the relationship has some descriptive failings and some serious normative failings. The paternalistic model of health care has been severely criticized in the past half-century or so. Paternalistic doctors may provide no worse care, but they provide it at a very serious price: patient autonomy rights. This brings up an important distinction in this OSCE: that between consequentialist and duty ethics. Consequentialists judge actions by consequences; if the consequences are good, the action is good, and vice versa. Many consequentialists would see little wrong with Cheung's behavior in this case because only good is done to the patient – the doctor is probably right in his assessments, and is probably even choosing treatment that brings the best results in the shortest time.

Judged, then, strictly by the consequences of his actions, he has been acting ethically. But duty ethicists would argue that the doctor has not been treating his patients as fully rational, capable people, and hence has been acting unethically. Resolution of these viewpoints might happen if we take a long-term perspective. It may be the case that giving placebos has more harmful than beneficial consequences if we consider the damage done to the medical profession. If Dr. Cheung's patients were to become aware of their deception, they might come to doubt the honesty and usefulness of doctors.

Paternalism, while no longer considered a good model of interaction, is necessary under certain circumstances. A paternalistic attitude is, of course, the only possible relationship in cases where a patient is incompetent, and it is sometimes recommended when the knowledge of a diagnosis might cause more harm than good. Paternalism and deception (both of which must be justified if we are to allow placebo use) might be allowable when the doctor cannot treat the patient as a capable person, when no harm will be done to the reputation of the profession, and when the benefits outweigh the harms. It is difficult to decide what action the applicant should take. Some options are: reporting Cheung to the college, speaking to him in private, and ignoring this minor transgression. In their quest to appear ethical, though, and especially in a trying environment such as this, people sometimes suffer from excessive piety. Applicants should, I think, have a more measured and considered response, one which is neither zealous nor laissez-faire. Perhaps the best solution is further consultation – the applicant, being relatively inexperienced, should probably seek out more professional opinions.

Short answers for the follow up questions:

A. What's wrong with the way Dr. Cheung treats his patients? Why is that wrong?

   a. Dr Cheung is treating all his patients paternalistically. This is acceptable in rare circumstances (when the patient is mentally incompetent), but not in most.

B. Why do you think Dr. Cheung does it?

   a. Dr. Cheung presumably does it because it leads to the best (short-term) consequences with the fewest difficulties.

C. Can you see any circumstances under which recommending a placebo might be the appropriate action?
   a. Recommending a placebo should probably only be done when no real medicine is suitable and:

      i. the doctor can't treat the patient as a capable person.

        ii. no long-term damage to her reputation will result

        iii. the benefits will outweigh the harms
- D. What is the difference between the applicant's previous response and Dr. Cheung's practice?
  a. Obvious
- E. What action would you take regarding Dr. Cheung?

    a. Measured and considered response–maybe more consultation.

Society or current events questions

There may be questions that are based on events that are important to the city and in the news a lot. For example, the city may be hosting the Olympics and in the news, there has been some debate over the compensation for winning gold medals for Canada and the question will probe your perspective on whether Canada should provide more funding or reward for winning medals for Canada. You need to be regularly reading the newspaper or watching the news to keep up to date on issues that are important in the city, country and world so that you will be prepared to comment on them or at least have a level of awareness of the issue in case they ask you. Reading news articles will provide a background and awareness of the issues. It is useful to regularly read the opinion articles in the newspaper and the letters to the editors to view different people's opinion on the topic to expand and to understand the arguments and perspectives on issues.

There are often questions on the health care system, areas of strength, areas for improvement, understanding of the Canadian health care system and comparing it to other health care systems in the world. You will need to understand the Canadian health care system and obtaining background information can be done through the Health Canada website where there are pdf documents describing the Canadian health care system. You will want to learn about the strengths, problems of the Canadian health care system and ideas proposed to improve the Canadian health care system. This can be done by searching websites, reading books, and being aware of news articles in the newspaper or magazines such as the Economists which often provides a good description of the problem and proposed solutions. For example, a major strength of the Canadian health care system is that universal health care is available to all citizens and is free at the point of use, but this leads to the problem of long wait lists and possibly untimely access to health care services. One proposed solution is based on the observations that waitlists are longer for some specialists than others and by moving patients from doctors with long waitlists to doctors with shorter waitlists, the waitlist times can be made to be more reasonable. In other words, a more efficient allocation of resources would resolve some of the problems. Another issue with the health care system is the escalating cost of drugs which is one of the fastest growing and most significant health care expenditure for the country. A possible solution may be for the country to purchase pharmaceuticals in bulk to gain bargaining power to negotiate lower costs and work with pharmaceutical companies. Another useful area to obtain a quick overview of the problems and solutions on health care systems are from videos on YouTube. There are many videos on YouTube that provides information on health care systems, problems and solutions, health care systems of different countries, and expert and people's opinions on the issue. The videos are often short, entertaining, and compresses a lot of important information in a multimedia format.

Spontaneous – creative questions

There will be creative questions that test your critical thinking. It will sometimes appear as if the exam question creator wanted to make a question that the interviewee will never think of and have them think on the spot. Usually, the questions are fun, and you can think of ideas on the spot. You must relax, let your ideas flow, grasp and expand on ideas that first come to your mind. An example of such a question would be choosing five things on a list of twenty things that you would bring if you are escaping from a sinking boat. You would need to explain your reasons for selecting certain items and forfeiting other items. There will be times in which the question will be scenario based and revolves around working with other people to enquire about your approach to resolving a problem. An example used by the University of Alberta that illustrates this type of question is:

> You and three friends are watching a 70-year-old man prepare a hot-air balloon. The balloon is ready, and the man is holding one of the 5 released anchor ropes which are all 6m long. His 10-year-old grandson is already in the balloon's basket. A gust of wind raises the balloon 2m off the ground. The man shouts for help and you and your friends each grab close to the end of one of the other anchor ropes. The balloon rises so high that even though you are holding onto the ropes, you are all lifted off the ground to a height of 7m.

> What would you do in this situation?

The follow up questions are:

A. What would be the first thing you would do in a situation like this?

B. What are the consequences of letting go and hanging on?

C. What would you expect your emotions to be immediately after you have made a decision?

D. How could this situation have been avoided?

In this question, a creative and fun scenario is created, and this may surprise inexperienced applicants. The thought process and logic of the answer is primarily being evaluated by the interviewer. Your values and priorities that guide your decisions will be noted. The way you function in a team may be evaluated depending on what is provided by your answer. Another question that places you in a creative situation that is in a more realistic setting is shown next.

> You are the shift supervisor at a MacDonald's fast food restaurant. The owner of the franchise has called you over. He is very upset as he has received 3 complaints in the last 30 mins. about the meat in the hamburgers being poorly cooked. There are two people (one male, one female, both 15 years-old) who have been cooking the meat for the hamburgers for the past two hours. The female is the owner's daughter.
>
> How would you handle this situation?

The follow up questions are:

A. What would be the first thing you would do in a situation like this?
B. What is the relevance of the female being the owner's daughter?
C. Is there a difference between how you would handle this situation in the short and long term?

D. Do you have any responsibility for the poorly cooked hamburgers?

You would need to manage and prioritize the issue of uncooked meat being a safety hazard to the customers, discussing and debriefing with the employees to find the reason for the uncooked meat and to make sure that it doesn't occur in the future, managing the relationship with the employees and the manager. The relationship of the daughter of the manager being an employee should not compromise your ability to provide safe food to the customer but should be dealt with tactfully to reassure and inform the manager that the employees were fairly and equally treated, and safety is a priority.

Getting to know you personally questions

There will be questions that are very open ended and are aimed at knowing more about you as a person. An example question may be, to ask you to describe the perfect day, what would you do and why does it make the day perfect for you? There is no right or wrong answer and the interviewer is simply trying to understand you better. These types of questions are generally very relaxed, and the interviewer is interested in listening to you share your interests, hobbies, and experiences.

Do you know the school questions

Sometimes the schools have a new program, new method of teaching or a vision that is unique to the school. The schools may ask questions to see if you are aware of the unique feature or aspect that is important to the school. For example, if the school has a campus or program in rural areas or wants to train more rural physicians, they may ask questions to probe your understanding of the rural program, understanding of small towns, and even ask you to weigh the strength and weaknesses of such a program, or the effectiveness of the program. If rural medicine is an important theme in the school, they may even ask for suggestions on providing patient care to rural areas.

Delivery of the questions

Direct Question

Most the questions are delivered by providing a preamble and asking a direct question. Sometimes the question is very simple or even a yes or no question despite a long preamble. In general, the interviewer will expand and ask deeper questions after you respond with your initial impressions of the question and preamble.

Interactive Chatting Questions

Due to criticisms of the lack of interactivity of some MMI questions that are based on direct questions by the interviewer and listening to the applicant answer with minimal response in attempt to standardize the interview; some schools such as the University of Alberta have introduced an interactive chatting type of question. The interactive chatting question is essentially a station in which the applicant will sit with an interviewer and chat generally. The interviewer is usually given some general questions in a list, but the interviewer has complete freedom to ask questions from the list or not ask any questions from the list and stray slightly to completely away from the list. The point of this type of question is to get to know the applicant and to look for salient problems with the applicant that may not be uncovered in a general MMI question. These questions are usually not graded, and the interviewer is simply trying to flag issues that may be important in terms of the suitability of the applicant as a physician. There really isn't anything you can do to prepare for such a question because it is essentially a small chat. You can try to develop of list of interesting things about yourself, practice talking about some of your hobbies and interests to help you get some practice, organize your thoughts, prepare some entertaining and insightful information for the interviewer so that you may standout as interesting, articulate, and unique from the other applicants.

Below are some example questions that would be in this category. The first set of questions is aimed at getting the candidate talking.

- Why do you want to be a clinician?
- Tell me about yourself.

The second set of question is given after you've had been through the MMI questions.

- How did that go?
- Have you had adequate opportunity to express yourself and show us who you are?
- Is there anything you would like to say to me that can be included with your interview today?

Interrogator and evaluator in the same room

Most questions are asked with a single interviewer and evaluated by the same interviewer. However, there are questions in which there are two interviewers in the same room. You will be introduced to the two interviewers. One interviewer will sit in front of you and ask questions while the other interviewer will be in the back observing, evaluating and won't say much but will be writing a lot in a notepad. Usually, the interviewer will ask ethics questions. Or the question may ask you to bring up an example to illustrate a problem and the interviewer will ask questions based on your response while the other person observes, takes notes, and evaluates. In general, you will only need to pay attention and maintain eye contact with the interviewer asking the question. You will only need to deal with the other interviewer when you enter and leave the room. The other interviewer will usually be too busy taking notes, evaluating and won't be providing much eye contact anyways.

Role Playing Questions

When you read the question on the piece of paper in front of the door, the preamble will look like a scenario-based question except there will be a note saying the question is a role playing question. The last sentence will say something to the effect that there will be a person in the room playing the role mentioned in the preamble and you are to respond and interact with this actor or actress. When you enter the room, you will generally meet an interviewer who is an evaluator. The evaluator will take notes in the background while you interact with the actor/actress. The actor/actress will be in the room and you will speak with the actor/actress. There may or may not be props, special make up or costume. The degree of acting can be very variable. The actor/actress may simply look like a medical student in plain clothes and would not resemble the character described in the question. For example, the preamble may describe a young teenager in a children's camp and the actor may be an adult with no attempt to resemble a teenager. The person may simply respond to what you say or not respond to what you say. On the other hand, some role-playing questions may be on the other end of the spectrum with hired professional actors/actresses, props and make up. Due to the range of possibilities, you should be prepared and not be surprised to encounter a role-playing question ranging from minimal acting to a dramatic acting scene.

An example of a role-playing question used by McMaster Medical Schools is:

> Your company needs both you and a co-worker (Sara, a colleague from another branch of the company) to attend a critical business meeting in San Diego. You have just arrived to drive Sara to the airport.
>
> Sara is in the room.

The history and background of the question is the role the actress plays in this question. The actress will play Sara, who is anxious regarding her safety. She had a friend who narrowly escaped being at the World Trade Center when it was destroyed. Until now, she had not experienced angst regarding air travel, but presumably there were latent feelings present, surfacing today with the immediate prospect of flying to San Diego. She had routinely travelled via air in the past, but this is the first-time air travel was required since September 11th, 2001. She is gripped with fear over what might happen.

The focus of the question is to create a station that is intended to be one that will allow an observer to evaluate the applicant's communication skills. The simulator should act in a standard manner for all applicants but should also be reactive to the approach taken by the applicant.

Below are some characteristics of effective communication skills that the applicant might display.

1. Listens well.
2. Remains supportive.

3. Avoids making light of Sara's concerns.

4. Normalizes concerns, noting that these feelings of anxiety have become quite common.

5. Confirms, without patronizing, that Sara is aware of the relative safety of air travel (e.g. better security now in place at airports, statistically tiny chance of being targeted, etc.)

6. Helps Sara separate the intellectual response of low danger from the emotional response of anxiety.

Summary of Types of Questions

The types of the questions covered by the MMI are:

- ethical – scenario-based questions
- society or current event questions
- spontaneous – creative questions
- getting to know you personally questions
- do you know the school questions

The questions can be delivered in the following forms:

- direct question
- interactive chatting
- interrogator and evaluator in the same room
- role playing questions

8. PREPARATION PRIOR TO INTERVIEW

Preparation for the MMI is very important in order to do well and feel confident. The earlier you prepare, the better you will feel and perform on the interview. Preparations should ideally start at least three months before the interview. There are also certain considerations and things you should do the last few days and on the day of the interview to ensure that you are in your peak performance for interview day.

Three months before the interview
The MMI is a type of interview that you can practice and prepare for the day. It will require more time to prepare because it involves practicing and getting into the mindset of answering MMI type of questions. There will be material that you can read to give you ideas and substance to talk about during the MMI that will be discussed later. The earlier you read the material the more time you will have to digest and to allow your mind to subconsciously blend it into being a part of you so that you can easily, casually and confidently bring up and use the information during

the interview. In addition, allotting more time will allow you to read more material and hopefully you will retain more information that you may be able to recall to answer questions in the interview.

Mock MMI Practice

The first mock MMI you try is to get an idea of the type of questions. You'll get to experience responding for eight minutes in a small room, reading and preparing a response to a question in two minutes. You'll also get used to the stress and stamina required to answer many questions in rapid succession. The first mock MMI should be video recorded and will serve as a baseline. The second mock MMI should be performed after you've prepared for the MMI and should be video recorded. After the second mock MMI, you will review the recordings and write down on a notepad all the strengths, things you did well, weaknesses and areas of improvements. Try to work on these areas of improvements and continue doing the things that were your strengths.

Mock MMI Simulation Conditions

Mock MMI exams are important to your preparation and should be done under MMI conditions as much as possible. The mock MMI should be performed in a room that most mimics the actual MMI room. You should find a small room, preferably with white walls and with few furnishings except for a small table and two chairs on either side of the table. Try posting the questions with a question per page on the door to the room. A tip would be to print each question on a separate piece of paper. Then clip or staple the stack of questions. Tape the stack of questions to the door. At the end of each question, simply rip the top sheet off to reveal the next question. Begin the interview by reading the question while standing in front of the door and enter the room after the two minutes and answer the question in the room. After answering the question and the time limit is over, leave the room and close the door to answer the next question posted on the door.

Training and Preparation at Home

The bulk of the training for the multiple mini interviews can be done at home as you practice, review material, and generate positive habits that will carry through on the day of the interview, so you don't need to pay attention to certain behaviors when you are stressed at the interview. Videotaping your practice interviews can be an invaluable tool to receive objective, private feedback and to monitor your progress. Videotaped interviews are an excellent tool to detect, help rectify distracting mannerisms and to check posture. Proper posture will help in providing a positive, confident first impression, proper breathing for better articulation. Posture is something that needs to be trained over time in order to be a subconscious and natural part of you on interview day.

Videotape Interview Practice

When you videotape yourself during practices, pay attention to filler words such as "uh", "um", "like", "so yeah", "you know." Minimizing the use of such filler words because it detracts from professionalism which something the interviewers are looking for in their evaluation. In addition, it detracts from communication of your ideas which is another factor the interviewers are evaluating. A method to give you an idea of the degree of the problem is to count the number of filler words in your video and work to minimize the tally of filler words with each practice. Mannerisms and unnecessary gestures should also be removed from your interviewing habits. A tip to pick up such mannerisms is to fast forward your videotape of your practice interview and these mannerisms will become very apparent. These mannerisms are very hard to correct because they are a part of your habit. You will most likely not be thinking of such things under the stress of the interview. Thinking about such things will hamper your interview performance. You should start early to give lots of time in your preparation to find these mannerisms through videotape practices and work on these mannerisms over time.

Posture

You should have a good posture while you are sitting and when you're standing because you will give a better impression, look and feel more confident. Good posture can be practiced at home so that on interview day you don't have to think about and worry about your posture. Thinking about and worrying about your posture will distract you from thinking, focusing on the question and add unnecessary stress. Practicing and training your body at home will generate a habit that will carry through to the interview. Doing posture exercises will also make you feel better and confident. Posture exercises has the added benefit of being a method to reduce stress accumulated in your daily life. A common exercise used for posture and relaxation in yoga is described below. This exercise is also used by actors/actresses.

Posture Exercise

The rag doll exercise will clear your mind, relax your body, and help you find a comfortable, straight-up posture. The rag doll exercise is done by first standing straight in a relaxed, upright position. Stand up tall and inhale as your raise your hands straight into the air above your head. Relax, exhale and lower your hands to your feet while keeping your legs straight. Be sure to release your neck so that it feels loose. While you are bent over, gently sway back and forth. Don't forget to breathe. Let your body hang in this position while you breathe deeply and slowly for at least five breaths. When you have relaxed into this position, gently begin to roll up from the back of your knees, through your buttocks, and all the way through your spine, one vertebra at a time. Continue to slowly raise your body one vertebra at a time and only raise your head when you have raised your shoulders. Once you are upright, be sure to take a deep breath and relax your shoulders on the exhale. The process of raising your body up should take at least 10 seconds. The position at the end of the rag doll exercises is the body's natural upright posture. Performing this exercise at least once a day daily will improve your posture.

Breathing

Breathing is essential to sustaining life and we've been breathing from the moment we were born and will continue to breathe until the day we die. Unfortunately, when we get anxious, we often forget to breathe properly. Learning to control and use your breathing constructively can be an enormous aid in times of stress. Breathing slowly and deeply can relax your body, clear your mind, and increase your ability to communicate effectively. A deep breathing exercise will be explained below.

Deep Breathing Exercise

Lie on your back and imagine that your body is melting into the floor. Take a deep breath in and exhale fully. Now, on the next inhalation place your hand on your stomach and see if it expands as you fill up with air. Keep taking deep breaths until you feel your stomach expanding on the inhale and contracting on the exhale. Close your eyes. Imagine that your body is a hollow vessel and that each breath you take travels from your head down to the soles of your feet. Don't rush through this experience. This is time that you've set aside for yourself to simply enjoy the feeling of breathing deeply. It should feel comfortable and relaxing. Stay on the floor, simply breathing, for at least five minutes. When you feel that you've experienced deep breathing and allowed your body to relax into it sufficiently, row to the right side of your body and rest your head on your right arm and rest your left arm on the right side and stay in that resting position for a minute. Then using your left hand push yourself slowly come into an upright sitting position. Stay in this position and continue to breathe deeply for at least a minute before getting to your feet. The deep breathing pattern in which you expand your stomach on the inhale, and contract on exhale is the most natural, efficient way for your body to breathe. With enough practice, this proper breathing technique will soon become second nature, and you'll find yourself speaking more comfortably and with greater confidence. In addition, performing deep breathing before the interview is very effective in keeping your mind clear and not wandering thinking of things that'll increase your anxiety. Deep breathing will decrease anxiety and help you remain relaxed when you are waiting to begin your interview.

Exercise

Regular exercise is good for maintaining good health and keeping you from getting sick. It is recommended that you engage in regular exercise at least three months before your interview. Do not suddenly start doing exercises within half a month of your interview as you will be placing stress on your body which will impair your performance on the interview. There may be a tendency to start exercising as you approach the interview to catch up on lost exercise time, or as something to do to improve your performance because you've exhausted all alternatives of preparation. But exercise needs to be done regularly for a period of time and cannot be crammed as many students have done prior to exams. You will probably have an irregular schedule for the few days surrounding your interview and may not be able to exercise at that time. Due to such practical limitations, it is probably better not to exercise for those days and if you manage to fit exercise in during those days, you should simply stretch or do yoga and treat that week as a rest or recovery week.

Two weeks before the interview

The last mock MMI, should be done within the last two weeks before the actual MMI and again should be video recorded. The last mock MMI should be done to most mimic the actual MMI conditions including the appearance of the room, the strict timing, and the process of entering and leaving the room per question.

Now when we review the performance of the last mock MMI, we'll be approaching the day of the real interview and it isn't the time for little details. The most valuable thing you can do for yourself now is to think of every good thing that happened during your mock interview and especially in terms of the progress you've made since your first mock interview. Think about what's there, not about what's not. Dwelling on negatives is strictly forbidden at this stage. When you finish the last mock MMI and review the video recordings, only look and write down the strengths of your mock interview. For at least five minutes, write everything that comes into your head in response to this question: What was good about what you just did?

9. Special Section for Applicants Flying Out of Town to Prepare Prior to the Interview

Many applicants will need to fly out of town to interview at different schools and there are many more preparations and considerations when leaving your home city. You want to minimize disruptions in order to have the smoothest interview and best conditions to help you perform at your peak on the day of your interview. That is the reason a special section has been dedicated to help you prepare and plan for your interview away from home. At the end of the section there is a list and description of essential things to bring or pack when flying for your interview to make each trip as easy and seamless as possible.

Preparation weeks before the interview

The moment you receive an interview offer, it is a good idea to book your hotels early because usually there are limited spaces and other students will be booking as well. It is not uncommon to have the hotels very vacant but full for the few days that interviews are being held at the university. The same goes for booking interview time slots if the school offers that as an option. Interview time slots are booked at an amazing rate, where a quarter of the spots may be filled within minutes of releasing the interview notice. In general, booking plane tickets early will give you a good deal as the prices tend to increase or the flight times become less appealing as the days tick closer to the actual interview date.

Preparation the day before the Interview

On the day before the interview, allow for time to relax. Prepare to feel confident and ready for the interview the next day. There is usually enough time to get an idea of the city, school and to do some explorations on your own. You will uncover interesting things that won't be covered by the tour of the school. It will also help you ask questions about the school and city. At the end of the day, you will have two necessities that will make you feel comfortable and help you start the next day fresh – and that would be a delicious dinner and a good night's rest. There will be some tips to help you make these two things happen as easily and smoothly as possible.

Getting to know the city of the medical school

If you arrive the day before the interview and you have time, I often like to experience the city or town. An efficient method to experience the city is by taking public transportation from the airport to the hotel. Taking the public transportation is a cost-effective method of transportation that reveals a lot about a city. It gives an idea of the quality of the public transportation, a chance to experience the city as a local resident, a chance to see the city, a possibility to talk to the locals and learn about the city and medical school from the locals' perspective.

It offers an adventure to learn a new public transportation system. The drawback of using public transportation is it requires preparatory work of researching the relevant bus schedules and maps from the city's public transportation website or Google Map. Extra steps for safety are recommended including having the hotel's contact information, map, and the taxi phone numbers for the city printed. Carry a cell phone in case you get lost on the way to the hotel. There are situations when public transportation is not recommended. Such situations include if the public transportation system of the town or city doesn't have a good connection from the airport to the hotel, if the city has a high crime rate, or flying into the city at a late time. If you're flying into the city late in the day, you will want to unpack, eat, shower, and get to sleep as early as possible.

Dinner

Finding dinner in certain cities can be difficult. The general concept is simplicity by being in control of the situation despite changing environments. One of the best places for food to keeping your condition consistent is to get food is at the airport. The airport invariably has a food court or fast food restaurants that provide a variety of low cost, quick, and convenient food. The moment you leave the airport, you are at risk of not knowing when you'll find another restaurant that you would want to eat and not knowing what kind of food or price. The food and beverage choice is usually healthy and simple to avoid food complications.

Sleep

Getting enough sleep is even more important when you are abroad. Adequate sleep is especially important when there is a change in time zone. Allocate about ten hours to sleep prior to your interview to ensure you've given yourself enough time to sleep. You may be jet lagged from flying in to your interview destination but the act of resting and lying on your bed in the dark for ten hours will ensure that you have attained the maximum amount of rest you can possibly achieve under your circumstances.

Setting a timer to wake up for the interview is important to wake up on time for the interview. Setting multiple timers is a better idea. Backup timers are important to avoid the situation in which a timer fails.

Preparations for the day of the interview

Breakfast

A simple, healthy breakfast near the place you live minimizes complications in the morning prior to the interview. Alternatively, bringing your own breakfast provides the ultimate control and convenience.

Plan the route to the interview location ahead of time. Book the taxi ahead of time. Arrive at the interview early.

Importance of water and health snacks

It is important stay hydrated throughout the day. Carry a bottle of water on the trip to the interview site and during interview. Bring fruits, granola bars or energy bars for a compact and convenient snack during the trip and on interview day. Many schools provide water, and some schools provide snacks on interview day. Bringing your own water and snack relieves your dependency on the school to provide hydration and nourishment.

After the interview

Remember to check-in for your flight back home.

A checklist of things to pack when traveling to an interview

Surgeons use checklists in the operating room to ensure they don't forget anything. You should use a checklist to ensure you don't forget anything when you pack for your trip for the interview. Forgetting to bring something can feel disastrous depending on the item and situation. Control everything you can to minimize unnecessary stresses and surprises that you don't need before your interview. For this reason, a checklist has been started for your convenience. Add and customize the list for yourself. Review the list when you pack and the night before your flight to ensure you didn't forget anything.

Checklist

- Interview day clothes
- ID (driver's license, passport)
- Pajamas, socks, and underwear
- Toiletries (toothbrush, toothpaste, deodorant, shaver, make-up)
- Medications
- Money
- Phone and charger
- Interview preparation material, pen, and paper
- Watch
- Water bottle
- Snacks

10. Preparation the day before the interview

Preparation before the interview is very important to ensure that you are at your peak condition. Prior to the interview, you should aim to sleep for ten hours. If you are not used to sleeping early to attain the ten hours of sleep, you should still at least by resting with your eyes closed to attempt to reach the ten hours of sleep and maximize your rest time prior to the interview.

At the end of the preparation and training, you've done everything you could do to prepare yourself for the MMI. You want to be relaxed so you can react to the spontaneous aspects of the MMI. So, the few days prior to the MMI should be used to relax and reward yourself for all the hard work you've done to prepare for the MMI. You should be applauded for getting this far in your preparation and application process. Since there's nobody to applaud your completion of a grueling training program, you must do something nice for yourself. It's a great way to relieve stress, remind yourself that you're worthy of special treatment, and puts you in the best condition for the MMI. Here are some suggestions:

- Take a bubble bath
- Get a massage
- Go out for a delicious meal
- Get someone to cook you a delicious meal
- Take a walk in a scenic area
- Read a short story
- Buy yourself some fresh flowers
- Rent a favorite old movie
- Take a nap
- Call someone you miss
- Have a fattening dessert
- Or do any other special thing you would enjoy

Remember, you must do at least one of these things and of course that's just the minimum requirement. It would be best to do them all.

11. What to wear for the multiple mini interview?

In an interview you want to dress relatively formal to show you respect the interviewer and to give a positive impression. You also don't want to stand out in a negative manner compared to everyone else. A safe route would be to dress conservatively and not stand out from everyone else. An alternative route would be to dress conservatively and modify the outfit by style or accessories to show something unique about you. This route can make you more memorable than everyone else or even give you a more positive impression than others. But the risk is if done poorly, it may give you a negative impression. In a traditional interview, making yourself more memorable has some advantages. But in an MMI, you are scored immediately after you finish answering your question and the interviewer doesn't think twice about you. The interviewer will not be evaluating you after those minutes you were in the room, so being more memorable does not give you an advantage. If you can make your outfit standout to produce a better positive impression than others, you would have an advantage but at the risk of producing a negative impression. Under the unknown subjective view of about a dozen different interviewers, it would be difficult to know that your unique ensemble produced a positive impression on every interviewer. Hence, barring superb fashion sense, a prudent approach is to select a conservative outfit that doesn't standout too much from other applicants. For men, this generally leaves them with two options. The first option is classically conservative dark suit and tie. The drawback of a dark suit is that it can be too serious and stifling. The next option for men is a blazer, dress pants, shirt and tie. This ensemble is versatile in the combination of color and designs and is less stifling and serious than a black suit. The second option gives the choice of relatively standing out from the other applicants while being respectful and formal at the same time.

Women have a wide selection of clothes they can choose from and they can be creative in their outfit. Women should still aim to be respectful and formal. Women can get away with a wide ensemble if it is not too revealing and relatively conservative. The classic two options many women often opt for are pant suits or blouse and skirt. In selecting a skirt, the skirt should not be shorter than knee height. Skirts can make an outfit formal and comfortable at the same time and adds variety to an outfit much like the blazer option for men.

12. The day of the interview

On the day of the interview, you'll probably be most nervous when you're waiting in the room with other applicants and culminates to the moment you stand in front of the door with your back to the question. Chances are, despite your preparation, you're still a little nervous. That's a good thing. If you were totally relaxed, you'd be asleep and that would not make for a good interview. The interviewers will understand that the interview will be stressful and especially the multiple mini interview. Staff and students will be there to make the MMI as smooth and stress-free as possible and cradle you between questions to make sure no one will get lost. They won't hold nervousness against you. It's a sign that you're taking the opportunity seriously. You can turn nervousness to your advantage. Channel the extra energy into the action of the interview. When you heart is pounding just a bit faster, your brain getting more blood. You're more alert and smarter than usual.

Here are a few tips to help you perform at your best on the day of your interview:

- Allow yourself plenty of time to get ready before leaving for the interview. You need to allocate enough time to comfortably get up, make breakfast, dress up, and commute to the interview location. You should have about 30 minutes of buffer time and arrive at the interview about 30 minutes early.
- Take your time getting dressed. Make certain you look your best so that you'll feel your best.
- Remember, if you've made it to the interview, you are a selected few and the medical schools want to meet you.
- Finally, know that you are now in the best possible physical and mental shape to succeed in this interview. The MMI is more fun than a standard panel or job interview. Enjoy yourself.

13. After the interview

Congratulations! You've completed the multiple mini interviews, and that's no easy task. During the interview, everyone was in the moment, consumed with the immediate concerns of completing the interview. Afterwards, now is the time for reflection. Keep a journal of your answers, progress, and questions asked after each interview to monitor your progress and to stimulate you to think and prepare for subsequent interviews. Think about what went well, and what didn't. Write in your journal for at least five minutes without stopping. What would you do the same in your next interview? What would you do differently? Did you present yourself in the best possible light? Did you communicate well? How did you do? The best time to do this while you are waiting for your way home, at home after the interview or if you flew away from home for the interview, while you're waiting for you flight home and during your flights. You can type away with your laptop or enjoy the intimacy of writing your reflections in a notebook or journal.

14. CONCLUSION

You've now been introduced to the style of multiple mini interview questions, have an idea of the experience of an MMI and preparations that'll give you confidence in completing your own MMI. There are some sample MMI questions near the end to give you a chance to tackle some questions in MMI format. Practice with more MMI questions to get used to the stress of a series of questions given in rapid succession and to help loosen your brain to react and respond the variety of MMI questions. Review the book as necessary while you prepare for the interview. Good luck in your multiple mini interviews and admission to a rewarding medical professional career.

FULL LENGTH MMI PRACTICE EXAM

Full Length MMI Practice Exam

Below is a sample multiple mini interview that mimics the type of question, duration and number of questions you would expect in an MMI. You should simulate the testing and room conditions described in this book.

Instructions:

There are eight questions. You have two minutes to read and think about the question and eight minutes to answer the question. Flip to the next page to view the prompting questions. Prompting questions are available on the next page and should be consulted when necessary. In the actual exam, the interviewer will read the prompting questions when you've finished answering or if you request the prompting questions. Interviewer score sheets are provided at the end of the book. Cut out the interviewer score sheets and give it to the interviewer to evaluate the interview.

Flip the page to begin.

Q1.

You are a sales associate at Future Shop and you are teaching two newly recruited sales associate to be knowledgeable about the products and to provide excellent customer service. Both sales associates reluctantly listen to you and are not motivated to learn about the products and make no effort to help the customers. You are expected to train them in three days and your performance in training these rookies may be rewarded with a promotion. One of the new sales associates is the daughter of the manager and the other new sales associate is her friend.

How would you handle this situation?

Q1 Prompting Questions

    A. What would be the first thing you would do in a situation like this?

    B. What is the relevance of the new employee being the manager's daughter?

    C. Is there a difference between how you would handle this situation in the short and long term?

    D. Do you have any responsibility for the poor performance of the new employees?

Q2.

Your uncle and auntie are in their late 40's and have been trying have a baby for the last twenty years. They've tried everything possible but were unable to conceive. Recently, a physician has developed a technique that will allow them to have five babies. They know you have a medical background and want to talk to you first.

How do you respond to your uncle?

Q2 Prompting Questions

A. What are the risks of operation?
B. What people involved in this situation?
C. How does your uncle feel?
D. How do the other people in this situation feel?
E. What factors do they need to consider?
F. What are the consequences of their decision?

Q3.

You are on a Caribbean cruise ship that sunk and escaped on a life raft. You are floating at sea on a life raft with enough room for three people. You have a box of food that takes up one passenger seat and you take up one seat, so you have room for another person. Your life raft floats towards two more people wearing life vests floating in the water. One of the people in the water is a 12-year-old child and the other is an elder person. There is only enough space on the boat to take up one passenger.

What would you do in this situation?

Q3 Prompting Questions

A. What are your options?
B. What other information do you want to know?
C. What emotions do you think each of the people involved is experiencing?
D. What would you do if you can only save one person?

Q4.

You are volunteering as one of the towel personnel for the diving competition at the Olympics. You've been diligently passing out towels to Olympians and enjoying the events. You have a towel in hand as usual and in the waiting area where the Olympic divers for Canada are waiting for their turn. You notice one of the Olympians started to cry. The Olympian is in the waiting room.

What would you do in this situation?

Q4 Prompting Questions

A. What would be the first thing you would do in a situation like this?
B. What are the consequences of him doing well or poorly?
C. How does the athlete feel?
D. What would you expect your emotions to be immediately after making your decision?
E. How could this situation be avoided?

Q5.

Your mother is suffering from a back injury and has unceasing chronic pain that hurts so much that she spends most of the time in bed and is taking higher doses of opioids that only take the edge of the pain. There is a procedure that can be performed to heal her injury and obfuscate her pain. The procedure will require waiting for two years in Canada. However, the same procedure can be done in India for $10,000 in the next few months. You do not have the money, but you are able to borrow from the bank for the procedure. You are against jumping the queue for wait lists, but you care for your mother a lot.

Would you have the procedure performed abroad?

Q5 Prompting Questions

A. Who is involved in making this decision?
B. What are some possible consequences of making their decision?
C. How do you feel about their decision?
D. How would your mother feel about the decision?
E. What factors do you need to consider?
F. How would you respond if your mother is hesitant about the operation?
G. Would you make the same decision if it was your friend's mother instead of your mother?

Q6.

Your roommate has been dating a girl for five years. His girlfriend has been obliging and has been doing most of the household chores and they've been living together for two years before he moved in with you for university. He had to move away from home for university and they've been maintaining a long-distance relationship by communicating online or for a few days or week at a time when he visits his parents. Suddenly, your roommate's girlfriend tells your roommate that she wants to break up and your roommate is devastated.

How would you respond to your roommate?

Q6 Prompting Questions

A. How does your roommate feel?
B. What are some of the reasons for sudden break up?
C. What are some options that your roommate can pursue?
D. What are the consequences of carrying out these options?
E. What can you do to help him?

Q7.

If, as part of the admissions process, we were to interview your best friend, what would they say about you?

Q7 Prompting Questions

A. What would they say would be best characteristic that you possess?
B. What would they say would be your weakness?
C. If you could change one thing about yourself, what would it be?

Q8.

A new medication introduced by a major drug company is supposed to be next revolutionary pain medication. Soon after the drug made the market, evidence demonstrated that the new pain medication has side effects that increase cardiovascular diseases such as heart attacks. As a result, the drug was removed from the market as an over the counter drug to a prescription drug. You are a family physician and a patient with severe chronic pain has been on this pain medication and is requesting to remain on this pain medication?

    Will continue to prescribe this pain medication?

Q8 Prompting Questions

A. How do you feel?
B. What options do you have in responding to the situation?
C. What actions would you take?
D. What factors do you need to consider?
E. How do you ensure the patient understands the risks?
F. If the patient understands the risks and strongly wants the pain medication because of the pain relief, will you prescribe the pain medication?
G. What are some considerations if you do prescribe the medication?

Comments for MMI Questions

Each MMI question is made to be open ended and can encompass a wide range of answers that are unique to each person. There are a few areas to note in providing your answers that will lead you to fulfill the points that interviewer is expecting and evaluating. These notes are provided for each of the questions in the practice interviews. At the end of the interview when you are reviewing your answers in your head and watching your answers on video, read the notes to ensure that you are on the right track and have incorporated the notes to provide the optimal answer.

- Q1. This question is an attempt to create a creative scenario that is not entirely foreign to the general applicant pool. This question tests your ability to prioritize and to create a plan under a stressful and time constrained environment. Factors that need to be balanced includes the teaching work ethic, teaching customer service, maintaining the company's reputation, methods to rectify the problem of lack of motivation, interpersonal skills in dealing with subordinates, communication skills that involve tact between you and your supervisor and subordinates, and justice and fairness in dealing with the consequences of improper action on the job.

- Q2. This question is an opportunity to demonstrate your empathy, diplomacy, persuasion and communication skills. Some people may be emotionally involved in this question. Maintaining composure, calmly analyzing and answering the question while at the same time being empathic, compassionate and understanding may be a challenge to some people. Age, culture, personality, commitment/drive for 20 years, other family members, ability to care for the children at such an old age, the children may not be able to experience a normal childhood because the father and mother will be too old to play sports and take them out, the cost to society of orphanage if the parents decide to abandon, the cost to the health care system if the techniques fails or have side effects. The technique is illegal in Canada but legal in the states. Your uncle and auntie are considering having the procedure done in the US. Another consideration is the cost for any side effects will be paid for by Canada even though it is not allowed in Canada and not by the US which was the country that performed the procedure.

Q3. Question 3 attempts to test your critical thinking skills and attention in reading the question. You can demonstrate your interpersonal skills, compassion, empathy, diplomacy and tact in your answer as you respond to the situation and make your decision. An ethical consideration may be lurking in your decision that you may need to deal with it if you or the interviewer brings it up. Added to the mix is the consideration of the different parties involved and their interests and the consequences that can severely impact the survival and group dynamics. There are several options some of them are innovative and requires some lateral thinking. One of the possible solutions is to recognize that you can have a person floating and hanging on the raft and take turns being in the water. Some people may consider throwing the food overboard in order to save another person, but this opens up the question of the group's ability to survive and how long they can survive without food. Some questions that might ask for more information could be to consider if the box of food can float or if the people can use the life vest to float the food or to tie the food to the raft using some of their clothes. These solutions do not need to exclude or choose a person to save. The applicant should note that they are in warm waters because they are in the Caribbean and both capsized passengers have life vest and are not in immediate danger of drowning. Since you are floating in a boat while they are floating in a life vest in warm water, they are not necessarily in greater danger than you. There are probably more immediate dangers such as the passengers starving or having an illness that would pose a more immediate risk that should be dealt with first. There are several factors that need to be considered before one can decide which person to save, including age, health of the two people, survival experience, the personal opinions of the two people themselves, and etc. Variations in these factors can significantly affect the survival of the people involved.

Q4. In this question, a creative scenario is created, and this may surprise inexperienced applicants. The thought process and logic of the answer is primarily being evaluated by the interviewer. Your values and priorities that guide your decisions will be noted. The Olympian is very nervous and under a lot of stress and pressure because the next dive will determine whether Canada will get a medal or not. He has been receiving a lot of pressure from his friends, family, teammates, and coaches to do well and is often told in the media to be expected to bring Canada medal from the Olympics. Second issue, the pressure is getting to him and a child hood fear of heights is causing him to tremble and he is afraid to go out and dive. A possible response could be to go and chat with the Olympian and demonstrate empathy and active listening. Offer comfort and encouragement. He has been diving for many years and has been able to suppress his childhood fear of heights and the emotion and the pressure now is giving him doubts. By providing compassion, empathy, and supporting him through encouragement and listening to him you will calm him down and he will emotionally de-escalate and be able to perform as he has flawlessly been diving for many years in preparation for the Olympics.

Q5. Question 5 involves ethical and personal considerations for the family. Your values of being against queue jumping is in conflict with your love for your mother and wanting to stop the pain and heal the injury so she can return to her normal life again and be free from pain. There is the risk of opioid addiction that will need to be resolved after the procedure as well as the impending opioid tolerance that will develop and may reach a point that it will no longer be a means for pain relief as the opioids no longer have an effect. In addition, the side effect of increasing opioid dose leads to poor lifestyle, compromised awareness and consciousness, and risk of death. The consequences of increasing opioid dose become increasingly important as time drags on as she waits for the procedure. The intolerable pain coupled with the risk of increasing opioid doses pose an unpalatable lifestyle and risk to her health. In addition, the financial cost of the procedure is significant and if you borrow money, you will need to pay off the interest and principal. The quality of the medical procedure abroad is a factor and any side effects or consequences of a poor procedure will result in the Canadian health care system paying and treating for the problems possibly created by procedures abroad. The home country paying for a procedure done in another country is not fair for the home country. However, the wait times are unreasonably long for the suffering patient. Faced with a difficult dilemma you may have feelings of conflict, torn, trapped, compelled, care and love for mother, upset that values might be compromised, and helpless in the health care system. It is reasonable for your mother to be scared and might be hesitant. Some possible factors that the mother may be anxious about and would need to consider include the safety of the procedure, side effects or potential consequences and the level of mental preparation of the mother and your ability to accept possible adverse consequences. Her anxiety may be diminished by informing the mother and noting the considerations and it will enable the person to make an informed decision that is most suitable to their values, lifestyle, and beliefs. Compassion, equality and fairness are being evaluated and may be revealed in the last prompting question.

Q6. Your ability to provide compassion, empathy, and communication skills are tested. The incident is traumatic to the roommate and he is devastated and overwhelmed with emotions that may include confusion for the sudden break up, pain or heartache from the break up, sadness when he realizes the loss of someone he cares about, self-pity if he begins to blame himself for his girlfriend leaving him, anger that his girlfriend left him, or despair if he believes that he won't find another girl who would be as perfect his ex-girlfriend. There may be a number of reasons for the sudden break up and this could be due to accumulated stress of a long-distance relationship that resulted in the last straw that broke the camel's back. There may be factors of under appreciation of the efforts or sacrifices made by the girlfriend. You can brainstorm reasons and possible solutions and options he can pursue, and this will engage his mind in searching for solutions and analysis. He may be emotionally overwhelmed and not ready to think and analyze the situation, in which case, more time will be needed for him to calm down and you can listen and empathize with him. Some possible options include encouraging him to communicate with his girlfriend to better understand the situation and act on more complete information or if he feels that stress of a long distance was placing a lot of strain on him too and may be considering with the thought of breaking up. If he wants to continue with the relationship he may be able to plan for the future with his girlfriend and salvage the relationship. On the other hand, if he chooses to break up it may be a tough decision for him to make but it may be better in the long term if there were deep rooted problems in their relationship. Sudden change in his relationship causes undue stress and is a risk factor for depression that may spiral in mental illness. He needs someone to be there, support him, and to talk and listen to him. You would empathize with him and actively listen. You may suggest he investigate counseling services offered by the university. You might try to engage him in social events to take his mind off things and to provide momentum to get over the break up.

Q7. A certain level of self-awareness is expected with the MMI and a lot of the MMI questions attempt to delve into you personally in an indirect manner. This question is considered a more direct approach to understand the applicant and is not usually encountered in the MMI. However, this question stimulates you to think about characteristics of yourself that you may be able to consciously make shine in other MMI scenarios.

Q8. In this question, an approach can begin by acknowledging the situation along with the existing complications and difficulties in the system and your best course of action and its limitations. A part of the MMI is being able to deal with ambiguities, uncertainties and creating a course of action that best incorporates the many factors involved in a complicated situation. Chronic pain is a severe problem for patients. Pain causes mental stress, can reduce lifestyle to something not more than being sedentary, which can cause a person to lose their identity if they can't enjoy doing something they value, can cripple social life, can prevent being able to work and these effects can spiral to depression and financial problems. In view of these life altering factors the patient may be willing to accept the risks to have pain relief and regain more control of their life. The physician might consider prescribing the pain medication and the physician must ensure the patient understands the risks and monitor the patient's condition.

Interviewer Scoring Sheets

Instructions:

Cut out the interviewer score sheets and give it to the interviewer to evaluate and grade your performance. The interviewer will provide a grade from a scale of 1 to 10 ranging from poor to excellent for each category and an overall score. Space is provided under each category to note areas of strength, challenges, and improvements.

Exam

Date: _____

Communication skills:

Question #:	1	2	3	4	5	6	7	8
Score (__/10)								

Strength of Arguments:

Question #:	1	2	3	4	5	6	7	8
Score (__/10)								

Suitability for Health Sciences:

Question #:	1	2	3	4	5	6	7	8
Score (__/10)								

Overall:

Question #:	1	2	3	4	5	6	7	8
Score (__/10)								

NOTES

www.ingramcontent.com/pod-product-compliance
Lightning Source LLC
Chambersburg PA
CBHW021357300426
44114CB00012B/1273